This Book Records Christmas
19

Name ________________________________

Address ________________________________

____

____

____

____

**This book is dedicated to Father Christmas
and his faithful reindeer.
Long may they ride through
the starlit sky on Christmas Eve.**

Christmas Record Book

Written by Barbara Hayes

Illustrated by Marilyn Day.

CONTENTS

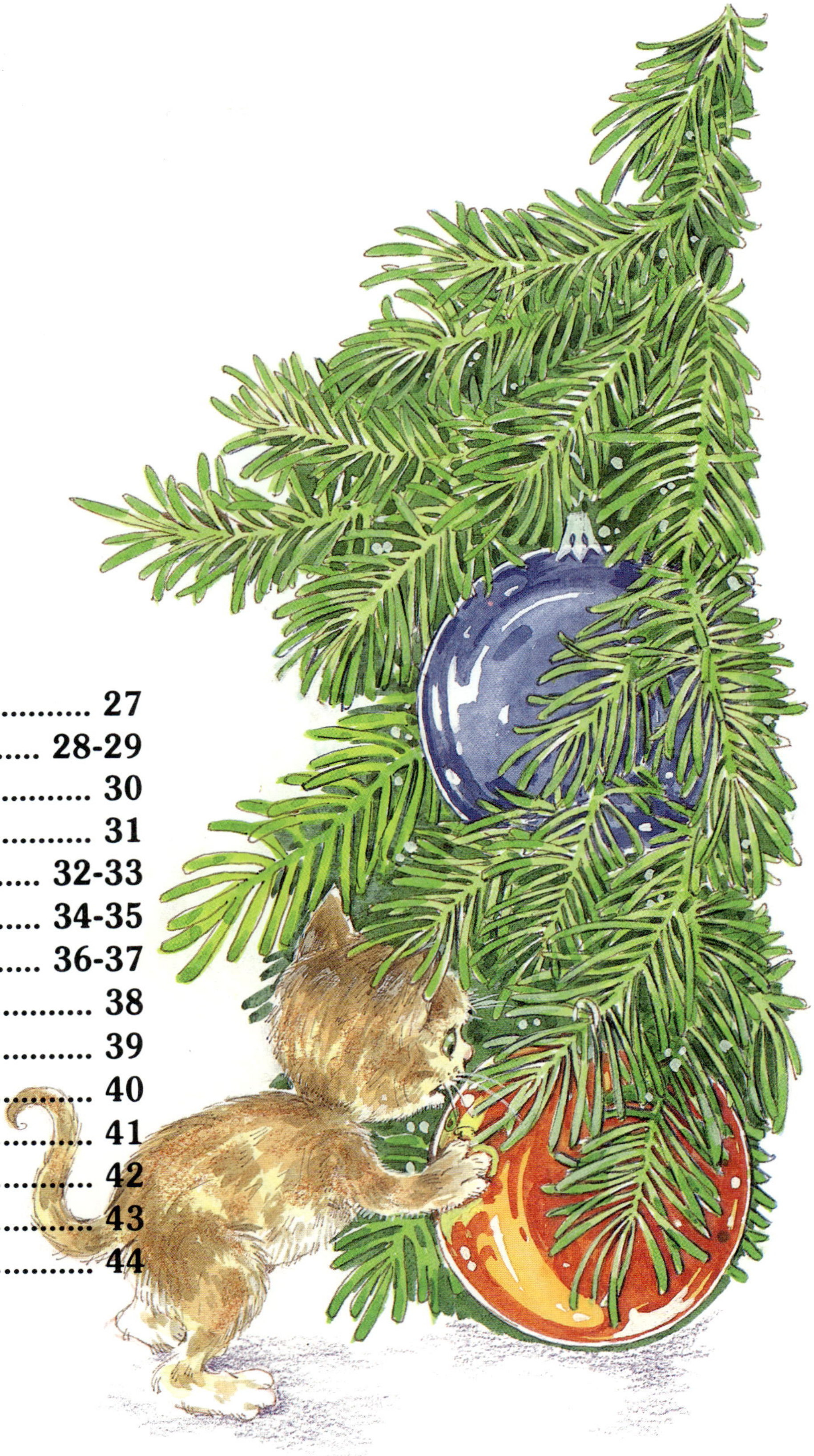

HAPPY CHRISTMAS!

This book is a place in which you may record your Christmas memories and also a place in which you may write all those lists and notes which ensure that Christmas is happy and that nothing is forgotten.

There are spaces for photographs, places for signatures of the family and friends, who share the festive season with you, places for Christmas card lists and Christmas present lists, places to note family clothes' sizes to ensure that Christmas gifts fit, and spaces for noting down successful recipes. There are a few fun pages to amuse those folk who need to sit quietly after a huge festive dinner. There is a ghost story to be read aloud with the lights turned down dim. Christmas is not Christmas without a ghost story! Nor have the little ones been forgotten. There is a story about Father Christmas to be read aloud to them. This is a family Christmas book for young and old. In years to come you will be able to take out this book and see who was with you in those days of happy memory. You will recall when the first slice of Christmas cake was cut and who squealed at the ghost story. Sadly some old faces will have departed, but darling new ones will have arrived and that is the way of the world.

SIGN IN FOR CHRISTMAS

Ask everyone who stays with you or visits you or with whom you visit over Christmas, to sign on this page. As the years go by, you move house, other people move house, jobs change, work colleagues drift away. In only a few years time you will look at this page and be amazed at who signed it - and who did not sign it! People unknown to you now, may be all important within a few brief months. In any case, ask your family to start signing while there is still space. It seems as if one silent visitor has signed while no one was looking!

WHERE WAS CHRISTMAS SPENT?

Was Christmas spent at home, staying with relatives for a day, for a night, for the whole holiday? Were brief visits made to friends or neighbours? Make a note of all the names and addresses. Maybe next year the hospitality ought to be returned - or perhaps not! You will want to remember and act accordingly!

PHOTOGRAPHS

Here is a space for photographs
of the people who celebrated Christmas with you.

CHRISTMAS CARD LIST

Write down the names of everyone to whom you sent Christmas cards. Then add the names of people who sent you cards, but are not on your list. You will find this page useful when you are mailing your cards in future years.

CHRISTMAS PRESENT LIST

Make a list of the names of people to whom you like to give presents. Always try to buy two spare Christmas presents, one small and one a little more substantial. Then, if you discover to your horror, you have forgotten someone, disaster is averted. The presents need not be wasted. They can be saved for birthday presents later.

Christmas Eve with Father Christmas

A story for the under-tens. During the approach to Christmas, younger members of the family can become over-tired and tearful. When this happens try to let everyone sit down for a rest, while a kind adult reads this story aloud.

Father Christmas and Mrs. Christmas and the elves and gnomes and fairies had been hard at work for weeks, but at last it was Christmas Eve. All the presents had been made and wrapped and loaded on to Father Christmas's large sledge. The reindeer were well-fed and strong, quite fit enough to pull the sledge on the long journey through the sky and round the world.

Father Christmas and Mrs. Christmas and their little helpers sat down for a well-deserved rest. The elves and gnomes and fairies ate the sandwiches and little iced cakes Mrs. Christmas put before them. They drank the hot fresh tea and the milk and lemonade. Father Christmas ate and drank nothing.

"You should eat something, Father Christmas," Mrs. Christmas said anxiously. "You know you are hungry and you have a long journey and lots of climbing in and out of the sledge with heavy loads of parcels ahead of you." Father Christmas smiled. "I am hungry," he said, "but I know all the little children all over the world will be leaving snacks out for me when they go to bed on Christmas Eve. I know I can rely on them to remember me and I do not want to disappoint them by not eating what they leave out."

One of the elves gulped down a lovely tomato and cucumber sandwich and as he reached for another one asked, "Don't you ever get tired of mince pies, Father Christmas? Mince pies are what the children always leave out for you, aren't they?"

"No," smiled Father Christmas. "I love mince pies. I enjoy every one I eat, but a change is always nice. If any children have no mince pies to spare and leave out a slice of cake, or a biscuit and some cheese or a sweet, that is very acceptable on a cold night's journey too. And if any children have no snacks to spare, then a little note saying 'Thank you, Santa!' will show that my work is appreciated."

A fairy looked up from eating an iced fairy cake.

"Why are you sometimes called Father Christmas and sometimes Santa?" she asked.

Father Christmas smiled again.

"We world travellers often have many different names," he replied. "We are called different things in different countries. In some places I am known as Saint Nicholas, which can be said as Santa Claus and then shortened to Santa. Anyway, enough of this chatting. It is time to go." He stood up and went outside his warm log home into the snowy forest. A team of elves dragged on their boots and thick coats and hurried out with him. They opened the door of the stable and ran the reindeer across to the loaded sledge, where they harnessed them and fed them some last knobs of sugar to give them strength for the journey.

"That's right," said Father Christmas. "The reindeer have a hard night ahead of them, but do not worry about them too much. Many children leave snacks for the reindeer too. Often a carrot or knob of sugar is left out with a note asking me to give it to the reindeer and much enjoyed they are too."

Father Christmas climbed on to the sledge, took up the reins and flew into the air with a jingling of bells. Mrs. Christmas waved from the warm, lighted doorway of their home.

"I will have a nice breakfast waiting for you," she said "and of course a lovely Christmas dinner later on."

Two little elves nudged each other.

"With luck we shall be eating Father Christmas's breakfast as well as our own," they smiled. "The little children in the world are so good and thoughtful. They always remember to leave snacks out for Father Christmas. By the time he comes home, he is too full to eat another thing."

The sledge and Father Christmas disappeared across the sky like a flash of light. They had to travel very fast because they had such a long way to go. That is why so few people ever see Father Christmas. He travels so swiftly, he is gone almost before he arrives.

Now here is something for all children to remember on Christmas Eve. If you expect a visit from Father Christmas, ask if you may leave a small snack for him and perhaps a carrot or sweet for the reindeer. In the hallway or near the Christmas tree are good places. Then go to bed and go to sleep, for Father Christmas cannot leave presents for children who are awake.

Remember Father Christmas sets out hungry and relies on snacks from the children of the world to keep him and his reindeer going.

Also remember that there are little elves back in Father Christmas Land looking forward to extra helpings of breakfast on Christmas morning. They are hoping Father Christmas will arrive home so full of food he will not be able to eat anything until dinner time and that his huge breakfast will be shared out amongst the others.

Start Christmas by making it happy for Father Christmas and his helpers and then carry on by being good tempered and well-behaved with everyone else.

Happy Christmas!

The End.

Happy Listeners

Sign on this page all who have listened to the Father Christmas story.
Little ones may make a cross or leave a finger-print.

Christmas Present Information

Make sure that all the presents you give are the right size and colour and to the taste of the person who receives them. Here is a page on which you can note down the size of slippers, socks, sweaters, pullovers, pyjamas, shirts etcetera of all your family and friends. Jot down which colours people like to wear. Note who likes plain chocolates and who likes milk. This information makes all the difference between a welcome and an unwelcome present.

PHOTOGRAPHS

Here is more space for photographs of your loved ones at Christmas.

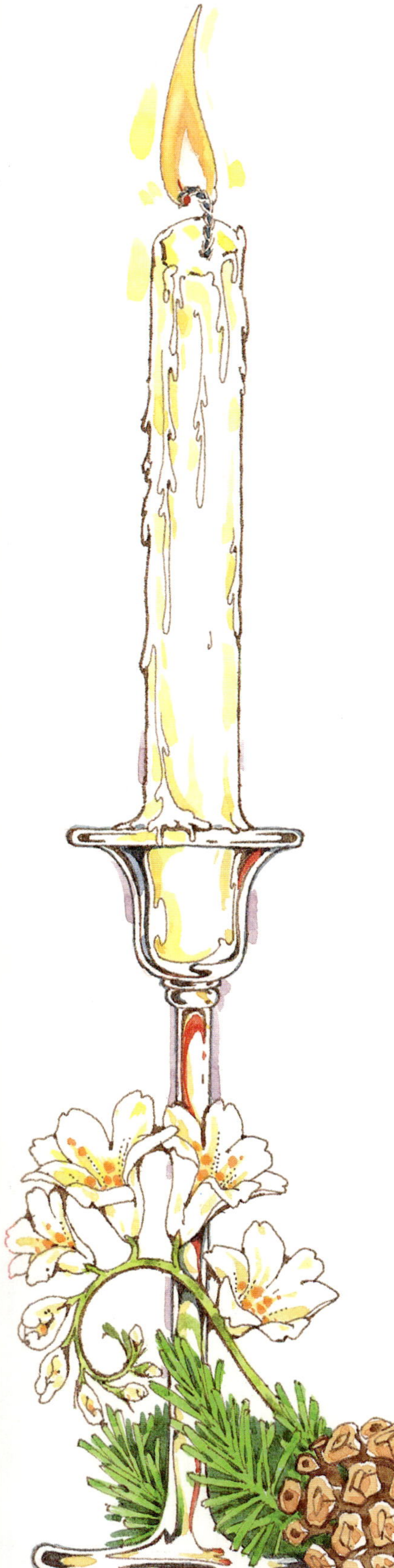

Grace before Christmas Dinner

Some people keep Christmas as a religious festival. Others hark back to the ancient celebrations of the Winter Solstice, when the Saxons decorated their dwellings with holly and ivy and the Druids brandished mistletoe in their sacred groves, when the Lord of Misrule walked the courts and palaces and much eating and drinking passed away the dark hours of the longest night of the year.

Whatever our beliefs, many people would like to pause before the indulgence of a generous Christmas dinner, to read out this short grace:

In this moment of quiet, we bow out heads to give thanks for all who are gathered together on this day. Long may we support and comfort each other through the trials of this world. We remember those who have departed from amongst us and give thanks for the time they were with us. We give thanks for the new little companions who have come to join our circle and wish them good fortune in the years to come.

We give thanks for all those who have worked to make this celebration possible and for the beautiful world in which we live.

For those rich or fortunate, for those poor or lonely, may this Christmas bring happiness into their lives.

Last, we give thanks for this magnificent dinner and may we all enjoy it as we deserve.

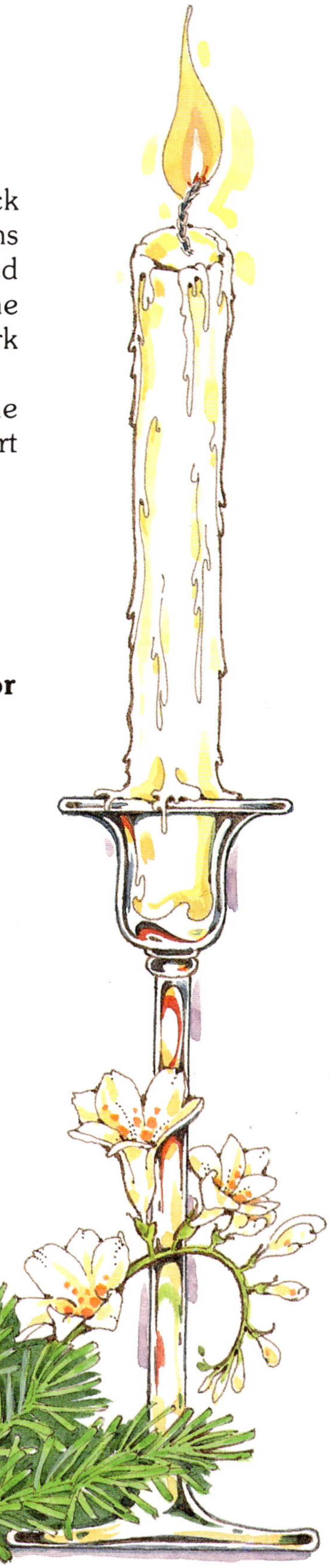

WHAT WE ATE

Here is a space in which to note down, a particularly successful recipe, or hints which made a dish better this year than usual. Was a different icing put on the Christmas cake? Was a new stuffing tried in the turkey? Jot down the menus of the meals you ate. It is surprising how even a traditional dinner can change over the years. Perhaps you went visiting and ate something different and tasty. Here is the place to note it all down to help you with your Christmas food next year.

PHOTOGRAPHS

Here is more space for those precious photographs. Look back in future years and see whose hair has turned white, who has become fatter or thinner, or smarter or balder or taller or more like their mother or the image of their father.

THE CHRISTMAS STORY

Christmas is a happy family holiday which brightens the dark days of winter. For many people it is also a religious festival to commemorate the birth of the baby Jesus.

Long, long ago in the city of Nazareth lived a young woman called Mary, who was to be married to a man named Joseph. One day the angel Gabriel appeared to Mary and told her that she would give birth to a baby to be named Jesus, who would be the son of God. Gabriel told Mary that her relative, Elizabeth, was also expecting a baby. This greatly surprised Mary, because Elizabeth was old. She hurried to visit her cousin and found that the news was indeed true. Elizabeth was six months pregnant with a baby who would become John the Baptist. When Elizabeth saw Mary, her baby leapt in her womb for joy and the Holy Spirit came upon them and told them that Mary's baby would be their Lord. Mary stayed with Elizabeth for some weeks and then returned to her own home.

Now it so happened that when the holy baby was due to be born, Joseph and Mary had to journey to a place called Bethlehem in order to be counted in a census ordered by the Roman emperor. Bethlehem was full of visitors, so full that Joseph and Mary had to take shelter in a stable because there was no room at the inn. It was here that the baby Jesus was born and his mother wrapped him in swaddling clothes and laid him in a manger. Out in the countryside nearby, some shepherds were keeping watch over their flocks by night. They were very frightened when an angel surrounded by a glowing light came and stood over them. The angel told them not to be afraid because he brought them tidings of great joy. He said that a baby who was their saviour had been born and was lying in the nearby city, cradled in a manger. Then a multitude of angels filled the sky praising God and wishing peace on earth to all men. When at last darkness fell once more over the hillside the shepherds hurried away to find the holy child and knelt at his side in wonder.

There were also at that time Wise Men journeying from the East. They had seen a star telling them that a new King of the Jews would be born and they had come to find him. This did not please Herod the king, who had no wish for anymore to take his place. He ordered the Wise Men to be brought before him and asked where this new king would be born. The Wise Men replied that it would be in Bethlehem of Judea, as had been foretold by the prophets. Then Herod let the Wise Men continue on their journey but told them that when they found the child they should return and inform him of his whereabouts so that he could worship him also.

So the Wise Men followed the bright star until it stood over the stable where the young child was. They rejoiced that their search was over and went in and bowed down and worshipped before the baby and its mother, Mary. Then they opened their treasure chests and gave Jesus presents of gold, frankincense and myrrh.

Meanwhile Herod was anxiously awaiting news of the baby who was to be a rival king, hoping to kill him as soon as he could find him. His plan was not to succeed. God warned the Wise Men in a dream that they were not to return to Herod and they went back to their own country by another route.

When the Wise Men had departed, an angel of the Lord appeared to Joseph and told him to take Mary and Jesus into Egypt where they stayed in safety until after the death of Herod. So the baby Jesus was able to live happily with his mother until the time came for him to do God's work and become the Saviour of Mankind.

What we drank

Here is a page where the sophisticates may care to note down the names of the wines which best complimented their gourmet cooking. It may be the page where at last Grandma will part with the secret recipe of her home-made lemonade, which everyone enjoys so much.

Perhaps a cousin can be persuaded to write down the ingredients of that punch which made his twenty-first birthday party go with such a swing.

Maybe an old uncle will say exactly how he makes tea so that it is always so hot and sparkling.

Or merely make a list of what was drunk over Christmas. Long years later you will look back and be amazed by your simplicity/ sophistication/good taste/strong-head/discriminating palate/ foolishness/long-suffering stomach or enthusiastic daring!

Phone Calls and Thank you Letters

Christmas is not always spent at home. Do not be caught without the phone numbers of distant loved-ones. Here is a page on which to write the names and phone numbers of anyone you wish to phone on Christmas Day.

Many people use Christmas phone calls to thank friends for Christmas presents. If you wish to write thank you letters, use this page to make a list of the people who have given you presents or given presents to young members of the family. In the excitement of present opening, youngsters do not always remember who gave them which.

Drawing Christmas Memories

Christmas dinner has been eaten. The presents have been opened. The energetic folk have been for their walk and returned. No one is ready to cut the Christmas cake. Now is the time for everyone to draw a Christmas Memory in the Christmas Book. Pass the book and a pencil round the dozing circle and ask everyone present to draw a picture in one of the squares and sign their work. The drawing can be a picture of Father Christmas, a drawing of anyone else in the room, the Christmas cake, the family pet, the house, a self-portrait - anything to provide a memory of this Christmas. Little folk can be helped by grown-ups.

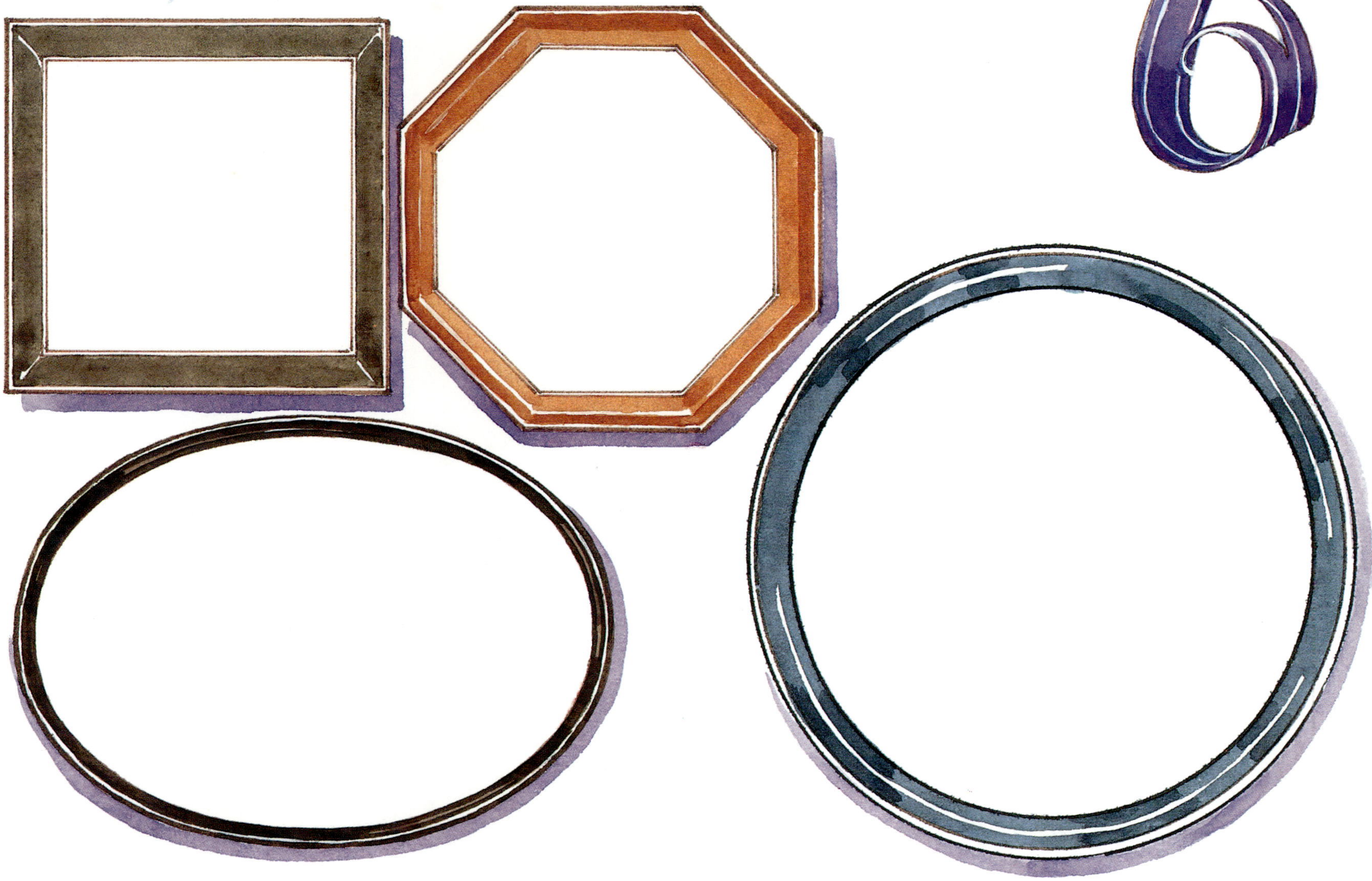

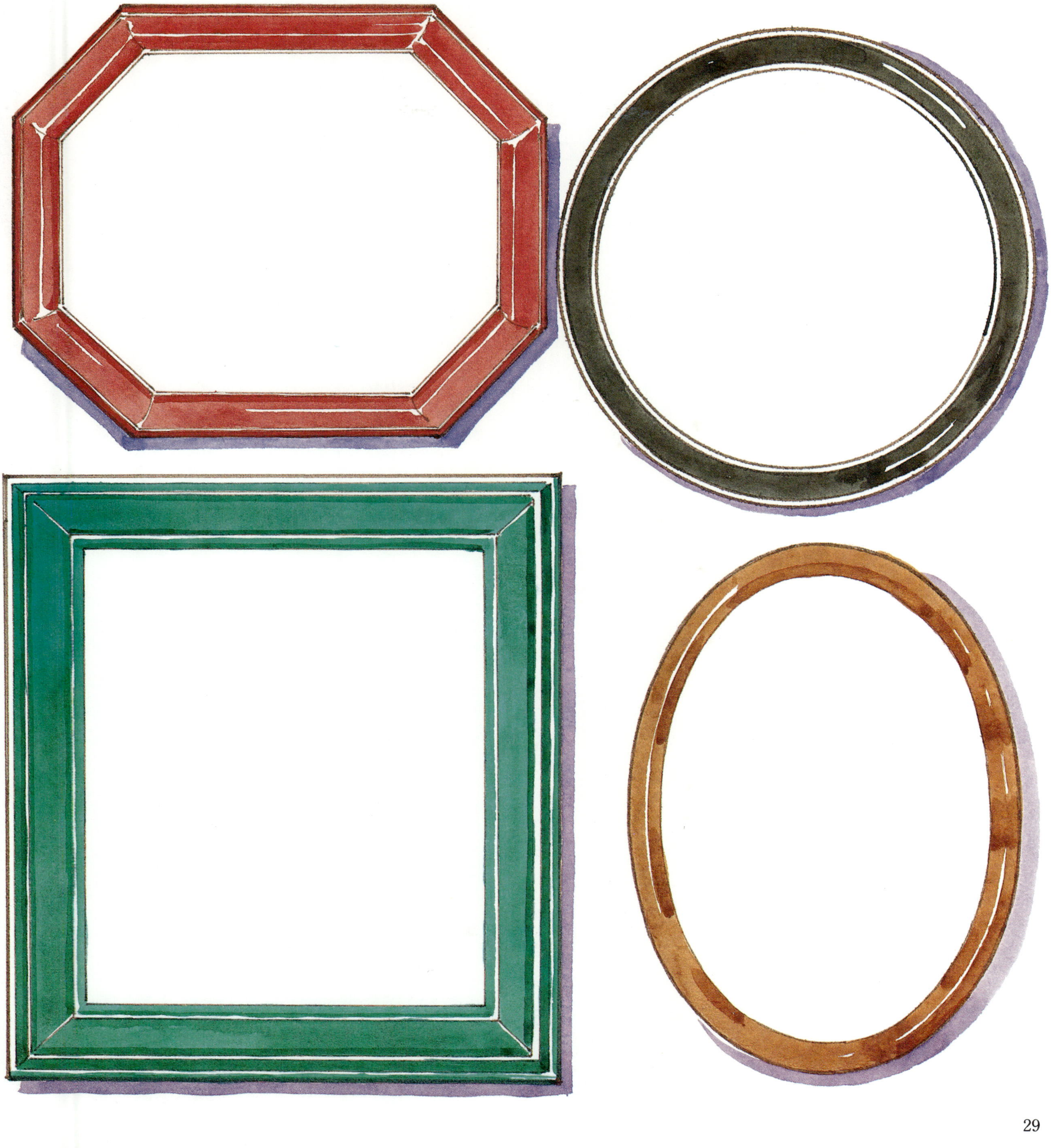

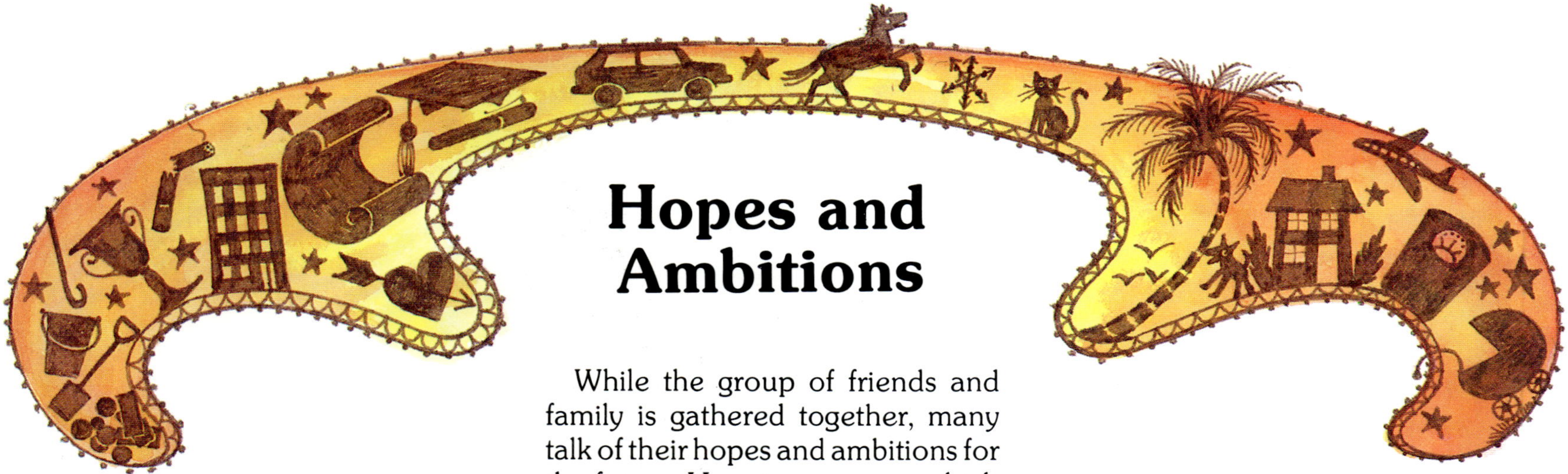

Hopes and Ambitions

While the group of friends and family is gathered together, many talk of their hopes and ambitions for the future. Here is a page on which those who wish can write down what they want for themselves in the coming year, what careers they hope to follow, where they wish to live, how much weight they would like to lose, what countries they hope to visit. We all like to dream our dreams.

Photographs

Here is more space for photographs. Why not take some of the exterior of the house or the garden? In years to come you will be amazed to look back and see how much they have changed. You may even be living somewhere quite different!

Night has fallen, the curtains have been drawn to shut out black, cold night. Only one light has been lit. Let the person with the bravest heart pick up this book, sit under the light, and read this story to those who dare listen. This is

THE CHRISTMAS GHOST STORY

It was Christmas Eve, the first Christmas Eve Charles and his family would spend in their new country home. Everything was organised.
Charles had left the office early and was driving home with the fresh turkey he had picked up from the farm. His wife, Samantha, had wanted a frozen turkey as usual. She said they tasted good, she could buy it beforehand and take it out and stuff it exactly when she wished and not endure a last minute hastle of work late on Christmas Eve.

Charles would have none of that. Now they were living in the country, they must eat country-fresh food. Nothing would taste as good as the fresh turkey he would order from the farm and bring home in plenty of time to be stuffed before the guests arrived.

Samantha's brother and parents were arriving on Christmas Eve to enjoy Christmas in the country in the new cottage.

Charles sat smugly behind the wheel. Here he was at a mere four o'clock in the afternoon driving home with time to spare. He turned up a small track which led to a deserted group of farm buildings. This was where he took the children walking on Sunday mornings. There was an abandoned orchard run wild. The apples were useless, but he had suddenly remembered that there was mistletoe growing on the trees. He would pick some to take home. Samantha liked paper decorations. They did not drop insects and juice over the carpets, but Charles believed in keeping up old traditions.

It was a cloudy evening and dark already. Charles stopped the car, slithered about through the mud, tore his sleeve on a branch, but cut a good supply of mistletoe heavy with waxy white berries. He turned the car to head back down the long, deserted track and the engine died. He groaned. What a time for a breakdown! Then he clutched his head. No petrol. NO PETROL! He had remembered everything else - the presents, the turkey, the mistletoe, but he had forgotten to fill up with petrol. He would have to walk home - ten miles by road - five miles if he continued along the rough trackway. If he walked back to the main road he might get a lift. He might not. Who would pick up a hitchhiker after dark? Only someone he would not want to be picked up by.

Charles decided to continue along the track. He took the turkey. He dared not arrive home without that. He took the mistletoe. He picked up the Christmas carrier bag of surprise presents. He locked the car and started to walk. There were no lights and only a fleeting moon. The track was muddy. Charles stumbled and slithered, grew cold and made slow progress. The turkey became heavier and heavier. Why hadn't he let Samantha buy a frozen one, as she had wanted?

He heard the screaming as he walked past the old farm buildings. Suddenly a blue painted naked figure brandishing a handful of mistletoe leapt in front of him.

"Give the word. Make the sign. Take the oath or die!" the blue demon shrieked, leaping round Charles in a circle. Then it stopped and looked at him more closely.

"You aren't Wayne," it said. "I was expecting Wayne to arrive. Who are you?"

Charles had not stopped, but had continued to hurry forward. Now he saw a bonfire beneath the shelter of a Dutch barn. Other blue painted figures danced in the warmth. Someone was cooking food on a barbecue. The first blue figure pulled a blanket round itself.

"Are you the police?" it said threateningly. "There's nothing wrong with acting at being Druids, you know. It's the ancient religion of the land. Druids were here first."

Charles continued to hurry on his way, hugging the turkey, the mistletoe and the presents. Trust his luck to run into a bunch of cranks who enjoyed painting themselves woad blue like the Ancient Britons and playing at Druids.

"My car has run out of petrol," he said. "I'm taking a short cut home. I'll leave you alone, if you leave me alone."

The blue demon became more friendly.

"You've got a long cold walk," he said. "I'll run you home if you wait till the ceremonies are over - but that won't be till after midnight."

Charles shook his head and strode

on. The sooner he got away from this group of madmen the better. Grown men who play at Druids on Christmas Eve could undoubtedly turn nasty if they thought someone might inform on them.

The remainder of his trudge was uneventful. It was cold and muddy and torn by brambles, but uneventful. He turned up the lane which led to his cottage. The porch light shone on several cars in the drive. His in-laws had already arrived. Samantha would not be pleased that she still had the turkey to stuff. He was about to turn into his gateway, when he heard hurrying footsteps behind him. He groaned. Surely not those insane Druids coming after him to make sure he kept his mouth shut.

He dumped his burdens inside his drive and turned. He saw Johnny Fellows.

"Johnny!" Charles voice was filled with surprise. Johnny had been his great friend at school. He had emigrated with his parents to Australia. They had not seen each other in years. "Johnny! What are you doing here? Have you come to visit me? Why didn't you tell me you were coming? How are you?"

Charles reached out his hand as Johnny Fellows came closer. Then he frowned with concern. Johnny was ashen pale. There was a streak of blood on his cheek.

Charles laughed. "Don't tell me your car broke down and you have been walking cross-country too."

"No. No. Nothing like that." Johnny's voice was hoarse. "I can't stay long. I wanted to see you - just to say hallo again, that's all. You remember when my people took me to Australia, when we were such friends, I said I would come back again to see you and the lads, but I never managed it. Well I've come now. Look after yourself, Charles. Have a good life!"

Johnny turned away. Charles could not understand him.

"Why are you going? You can't come all this way and not come in for a drink. Come to meet my wife and the children."

"No. No." Johnny's voice faded as he melted away into the darkness and he was gone. There was nothing for Charles to do but pick up his parcels, and go indoors.

Samantha was not best pleased with the late arrival of the turkey. His brother-in-law jeered at the story of the forgotten petrol and the mad Druids. He insisted that Charles had stayed for too many drinks with the boys and was making flimsy excuses. His story about seeing Johnny Fellows met with equal disbelief. Who would come visiting from Australia and not step indoors for a drink?

"That doesn't sound like any Australian I have ever met!" the brother-in-law derided.

The next day when everyone had mellowed and Charles was sipping a pre-turkey dry sherry, his mother-in-law switched on her portable radio. She never missed the news bulletins, even on Christmas Day.

"I don't know why you switch the news on," said Samantha. "There are always tragedies at Christmas and I don't want to hear about them."

Samantha was right. There had been an air crash in Australia. A light plane had come down in the bush and the pilot and his passenger had been killed. The name of the pilot was Johnny Fellows, an Englishman who had emigrated with his parents ten years before. Charles put down his sherry. Samantha and his brother-in-law stared at him.

"Who was that you saw last night, then?" asked Samantha.

Charles felt cold. "That was Johnny," he said, "come back to see me again as he said he would."

There was a silence.

"You must have been mistaken," said Samantha.

"I wasn't," said Charles. "I saw Johnny."

The children came in saying they were hungry.

"I don't see why we should let a ghost spoil a good Christmas dinner," said Samantha's brother.

For once he was right. The dinner was much enjoyed by the others, but Charles hardly tasted it. He had seen a ghost, that was sure and certain. His dying friend had come back across the miles and the seas for one last visit to his homeland and his old friend. And now he had gone where? Perhaps one day Charles would find out.

FAMILY FAVOURITES

We all have favourite t.v. shows, celebrities, politicians, royalty, colours and so on. Keep the younger members of the gathering (and the older members, who are young at heart) amused by voting to answer these questions. On the left hand page fill in the name of the show or person, who gets the most votes from the festive circle. On the right hand page fill in the names of those who voted yes and those who voted no. In years to come you will look back with amazement to see the things you liked.

Favourite t.v. show ....

Favourite film this year ....

Favourite child member of any royal family ....

Favourite adult member of any royal family ....

Favourite politician ....

Favourite actor ....

Favourite actress ....

Favourite t.v. news reader ....

Favourite pop group ....

Favourite male singer ....

Favourite female singer ....

Favourite colour ....

Favourite flower ....

Favourite meal at Christmastime ....

Favourite meal at any time ....

Favourite drink with Christmas dinner ....

Favourite drink at any time ....

Favourite car (money no object) ....

Favourite place to live (money to object) ....

Favourite holiday spot (money no object) ....

FACT SHEET

Sometimes our memory plays tricks, especially over who did the work. Just for the record

Who cooked the Christmas dinner? ....

Who helped prepare Christmas dinner? ....

Who laid the table? ....

Who baked the Christmas cake? ....

Who iced the Christmas cake? ....

Who made the Christmas pudding? ....

Who made the mince pies? ....

Who put up the decorations? ....

Who dressed the Christmas tree? ....

Who went carol singing? ....

Who went to church? ....

Who took the dog for a walk? ....

What time did the children wake in the morning? ....

When was the first slice of Christmas cake eaten? ....

Who ate it? ....

How many days did the turkey last? ....

Was it a white Christmas? ....

Do you want to record any other special happening? ....

LOOT!

Make lists of everything the members of the Christmas gathering and your family were given for Christmas. This will be a great help with choosing presents next year. Younger family members usually enjoy compiling this information.

MORE LOOT!

If you have a large family and circle of friends, you will need this page also for the list of presents. If your family is small, use this page for more photographs, Christmas recipes or even for sticking in knitting patterns of gifts which were warmly welcomed and could be repeated.

HEIGHT AND WEIGHT RECORD

This page is for younger members of the family and for those grown-ups who volunteer willingly.

Write in name, height, weight (and age if you are under sixteen). Those still growing up will be interested to see how much taller they are by next Christmas.

Those brave adults who fill in details on this page may smile with triumph if they are slimmer (or plumper according to desire) by the time a year has slipped away and, hopefully, the family is gathered together for another Christmas.

BABY PAGE

This is a page for those fortunate families with babies and toddlers still cuddled amongst them. The special baby words can be all too easily forgotten. Record here the baby talk your little ones use this Christmas. Do they say Bowaa instead of Bow-wow. Do they lisp Bunningrassit, instead of Bunny Rabbit? Did they manage to say Happy Christmas. Can the babies crawl? Can the toddlers walk? How far can they go? Record all the memories here or fill the page with Christmas photographs of the family babies.

ACHIEVING PERFECTION NEXT CHRISTMAS

However successful Christmas has been, there are always little improvements which could be made. Perhaps a cousin has become allergic to seafood and an alternative hors d'oevre should have been provided. Perhaps one of the little folk will not eat anything without tomato ketchup on it and a bottle should be kept in the house. Perhaps some teenagers have become vegetarian and the larder should be stocked accordingly. Make a note of all these things for a smoother Christmas next year.

And MAKE A NOTE OF WHERE YOU STORE AWAY THE CHRISTMAS DECORATIONS. Hunting frantically through the attic on Christmas Eve does not make a cool hostess!

NEXT YEAR'S CHRISTMAS PRESENTS

Thinking of Christmas presents to give is always a headache. Ask everyone who visits over Christmas to write down their names and as many things they can think of that they would like to receive as presents next year. All presents, except one, must be within the price range members of the family can afford. One dream present can be what would be chosen if price were no object. These pages should be very helpful in the weeks preceeding next Christmas and will also be a valuable social document for any historian who discovers this book in an attic hundreds of years hence.

HEROES AND HEROINES

Not all Christmas tasks are delightful. All that feasting generates mountains of washing up.

Sign in here all those heroes and heroines who volunteered to wash up the dirty dishes, who scraped the fat out of the baking tins, who scoured out the saucepans, who rubbed the cutlery free of stains and best of all, those who put the clean dishes and utensils away in the correct drawers and cupboards!

Write your names with pride to be remembered as standing in the front line of those who made the festivities a success.

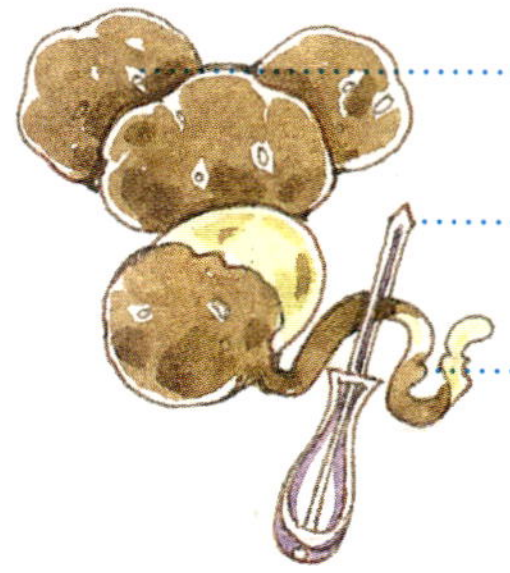

A
VERY HAPPY
CHRISTMAS
EVERYONE